THE OFFICIAL
West Ham United
ANNUAL 2010

Written by Rob Pritchard

A Grange Publication

© 2009. Published by Grange Communications Ltd., Edinburgh, under licence from West Ham United Football Club. Printed in the EU.

Photographs © West Ham United Football Club

ISBN 978-1-906211-92-9

£6.99

CARLTON COLE

CONTENTS

Welcome from Gianfranco Zola

First of all, I would like to welcome you to West Ham United's Official 2010 Annual and would like to thank you all for your continued support.

The reaction I have had from West Ham fans since I joined the club has been far beyond anything I could have possibly hoped for when I first arrived in September 2008. Every single supporter I have met has welcomed me in such a positive way and given my staff and players nothing but encouragement.

I know how much you give to this club and I can promise you that we are all determined to make 2010 a fantastic year and give you even more reason to be excited about the future.

We have a fantastic squad with the right balance of young players to go with our experienced internationals and it gives me so much pleasure to work with such a talented group every day on the training ground at Chadwell Heath.

I was not sure whether as a coach you could match the feeling you get as a player but I can say that I take so much satisfaction watching the team play well in front of a full Boleyn Ground.

Our goal this year is to improve in every way and I am sure we can do this, especially with the lessons learned so far. This is a great club and together we can help to make it even greater.

Thank you all again and enjoy your 2010!

Gianfranco Zola

HAMMER OF THE YEAR

SCOTT PARKER

West Ham United and England midfielder Scott Parker capped a fine 2008/09 season by being voted Hammer of the Year by the club's supporters.

An all-action player who never shies away from a challenge and is willing to put his body on the line for the West Ham cause, Parker has been a revelation since joining the club from Newcastle United in June 2007.

In 2008/09, Parker led from the front, making 32 appearances in all competitions and leading the charge as the Hammers secured a more than respectable ninth-place finish in the Barclays Premier League table.

The Lambeth-born player was delighted to receive the endorsement of the club's fans in the shape of his first Hammer of the Year award.

"It is fantastic. It is a great achievement for me personally and I am honoured to have won. It is particularly pleasing to have won an award voted by your own fans. It is a great achievement for me and I am absolutely ecstatic.

"It is pleasing if people think I am putting in hard work and giving my all. I don't know that myself because that is just the way I play. I understand I have an attitude to my game that the West Ham fans seem to like."

Parker's efforts were also recognised by a host of supporters' groups from across the world, many of whom attended the final home match of the season against Middlesbrough to present the player with his various awards. Among those to honour the midfielder were the Scandinavian Hammers and the Swedish Hammers Supporters Club, each of whom handed over attractive trophies to the popular Parker. In typically modest fashion, the midfielder was quick to pass on the accolades to his West Ham team-mates.

"I would not have won it, or done well this season, without my team-mates and the support of the manager. Everyone this year has been fantastic. There were many candidates. I am sure it was a close decision but I am over the moon that it is me."

An experienced professional, Parker began his career at Charlton Athletic before moving to Chelsea for £10m in January 2004. He would end the 2003/04 season by being named as the PFA Young Player of the Year.

After 18 months at Stamford Bridge, Parker moved north to join Newcastle United, where he became captain, leading the Magpies to UEFA Intertoto Cup success in the summer of 2006.

Parker moved back to London a year later, joining West Ham on a five-year contract. Since then, he has become a firm crowd favourite with his wholehearted approach to every match that he appears in.

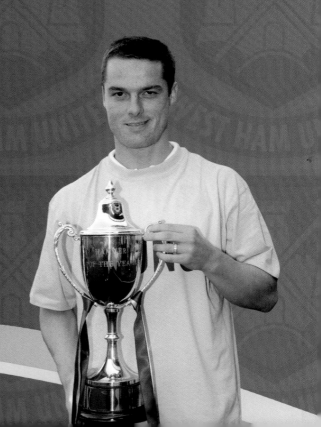

YOUNG HAMMER OF THE YEAR

JACK COLLISON

2008/09 was quite a season for Jack Collison.

The West Ham United and Wales midfielder scored on his home debut for the Hammers before establishing himself in Gianfranco Zola's starting eleven. Despite the frustration of missing two months of the campaign after suffering a dislocated kneecap in March 2009, Collison made a triumphant return before being named Young Hammer of the Year by Academy Director Tony Carr.

For Collison, the opportunity to shine only came about following an injury to fellow Academy graduate and friend Mark Noble. The youngster was drafted into Zola's squad for the Barclays Premier League trip to Manchester United on 29 October 2008, impressing as a substitute at Old Trafford. From then on, he never looked back.

Collison, who made his Wales debut in a friendly with Iceland in May 2008, ended the season

with 24 first-team appearances and three goals to his name, opening his account with a spectacular curling shot against Everton on 8 November 2008.

Amazingly, Collison may never have had a chance to impress had a loan move to League One promotion-chasers Peterborough United gone through shortly before his superb display at Manchester United.

"I did get a chance to go out on loan and then Mark Noble picked up an injury and I got an opportunity at Old Trafford," said Collison. "I haven't looked back and I've enjoyed playing my part in the team."

Now a regular for club and country, Collison is aiming to continue his improvement under the direction of Zola and his coaching staff. The player himself credits the manager for the huge strides forward he has made over the past 18 months.

"For me personally it has had a lot to do with the new manager coming in. I think he's come in and been brilliant. He's given us the opportunity to go out there and play with freedom and belief and to try things and not to worry if they don't work."

DORIS BELL AWARD

JUNIOR STANISLAS

Junior Stanislas was a deserving winner of the Doris Bell Award after enjoying a fine first season as part of the West Ham United first-team squad.

The skilful winger began the season as a regular in the club's reserve side before a loan spell at League One outfit Southend United served as a catalyst for him to make his Barclays Premier League breakthrough.

Stanislas, who joined the Hammers at the age of ten, appeared in the MLS All-Star Game in July 2008 before leaving for Southend in November the same year. After scoring twice on his debut in an FA Cup second round win over Luton Town, the youngster impressed as the Shrimpers pushed Chelsea all the way in the third round.

On his return to West Ham, Stanislas netted a hat-trick in a behind-closed-doors friendly with Chelsea, impressing manager Gianfranco Zola.

After being handed his debut in the goalless draw with West Bromwich Albion at the Boleyn Ground on 16 March 2009, Stanislas netted his first goal for the club on his full debut, scoring the opener in a 2-0 home win over Sunderland three weeks later.

Stanislas went on to make a total of nine Barclays Premier League appearances for West Ham in Season 2008/09, earning praise from Zola and scoring his second goal in the final day win over Middlesbrough.

At international level, Stanislas was also rewarded for his fine form with a call-up to the England Under-20 side, appearing in the win over Italy at Loftus Road in March 2009.

His maiden season as a West Ham United player ended with Stanislas receiving the Doris Bell Award, which is named in honour of the late Hammers fan Doris Bell and awarded to the player who has shown a great deal of promise over the previous campaign.

WORDSEARCH

CAN YOU FIND THE HIDDEN WORDS IN THE GRID BELOW?

```
P T C Z D Z K D T J P O C E
B R O O K I N G E B I C O T
C B B R E P P R C N C L L E
K J O S X J O L A C Y A L Z
C F L T Q O L C B O S R I W
A D E Q M E I I Z L J K S N
R L Y W F D M B F E C E O B
R D N F C O T T E E H V N E
H C U S T A N I S L A S I H
U R T P A R K E S N M A L R
R K B O N D S Z O I M V U A
S C W A T S O N K F E C N M
T U Q P A R K E R P R Q G I
X T O M K I N S P S S H A P
```

BEHRAMI	CARR	COTTEE	ILUNGA	RUFFELL
BOLEYN	CLARKE	DI CANIO	MOORE	STANISLAS
BONDS	COLE	HAMMERS	PARKER	TOMKINS
BROOKING	COLLISON	HURST	PARKES	WATSON

ANSWERS ON PAGE 60

ROBERT GREEN

2008/09 SEASON REVIEW

PRE-SEASON

17 JULY 2008

Hampton and Richmond Borough 2
Quarm
Yaku

West Ham United 4
Bellamy 2
Noble
Hines

West Ham United kicked off their pre-season programme with a trip to Blue Square South Hampton and Richmond Borough, managed by ex-Hammers midfielder Alan Devonshire. Francis Quarm volleyed the hosts into a shock lead before two goals from Craig Bellamy and one from Mark Noble restored order. Lawrence Yaku pulled one back before Zavon Hines made the game safe.

19 JULY 2008

Billericay Town 0

West Ham United XI 1
Hines (pen)

20 JULY 2008

Columbus Crew 1
Garey

West Ham United 3
Ashton
Evans (og)
Reid

Dean Ashton scored his first goal in a year as West Ham United beat MLS side Columbus Crew in Ohio. Jason Garey equalised for Columbus before a Brad Evans own-goal and a Kyel Reid strike settled matters.

24 JULY 2008 – MLS ALL-STAR GAME

MLS All Stars 3
Gomez
Blanco
De Rosario (pen)

West Ham United 2
Ashton 2

David Beckham's MLS All-Stars proved just too strong in an entertaining contest at Toronto FC's BMO Field. Dean Ashton scored twice for West Ham United, but goals from Christian Gomez, Cuauhtemoc Blanco and Dwayne De Rosario condemned the Hammers to defeat.

26 JULY 2008

Thurrock 0

West Ham United XI 3
Hines (pen)
Sears
Young (og)

29 JULY 2008

Peterborough United 0

West Ham United 2
Bellamy 2

Valon Behrami made his West Ham United debut as Craig Bellamy netted twice in a 2-0 victory at League One Peterborough United.

30 JULY 2008

Cambridge United 0

West Ham United XI 0

1 August 2008

Southampton 2
McGoldrick 2

West Ham United 2
Davenport
Hines

Calum Davenport and Zavon Hines rescued West Ham United after David McGoldrick's brace had given Coca-Cola Championship Southampton an early 2-0 lead at St Mary's.

2 August 2008

Grays Athletic 2
Welsh
Ide

West Ham United XI 1
Hines (pen)

4 August 2008

Ipswich Town 3
Shumlikoski
Garvan
Lee

West Ham United 5
Ashton 3
Bellamy
Noble

A Dean Ashton hat-trick was the highlight of a thrilling game at Coca-Cola Championship Ipswich Town. Craig Bellamy and Mark Noble were also on target.

9 August 2008

West Ham United 1
Cole

Villarreal CF 1
Cazorla

West Ham United legend Bobby Moore OBE's famous No6 shirt was retired on an emotional afternoon at the Boleyn Ground as the Hammers shared the inaugural Bobby Moore Cup with Spaniards Villarreal.

11 August 2008

Tilbury 0

West Ham United XI 3
Jeffery
Stanislas
Edgar

SEASON 2008/09
AUGUST 2008

16 AUGUST 2008 – BARCLAYS PREMIER LEAGUE

West Ham United 2
Ashton 2

Wigan Athletic 1
Zaki

Dean Ashton lashed in an early brace to get West Ham United's Barclays Premier League campaign off to a flying start at the Boleyn Ground. The England striker scored twice in the opening ten minutes before Egyptian Amr Zaki set up a tense second half with a fine volley. Valon Behrami made his debut for the Hammers.

24 AUGUST 2008 – BARCLAYS PREMIER LEAGUE

Manchester City 3
Sturridge
Elano 2

West Ham United 0

Three second-half goals in the space of eleven minutes ensured ten-man West Ham United would suffer their first Barclays Premier League defeat of the season at Manchester City. Mark Noble was sent-off on 38 minutes before Daniel Sturridge and Elano, who scored twice, put the game beyond West Ham.

27 AUGUST 2008 – CARLING CUP SECOND ROUND

West Ham United 4
Bowyer
Cole
Hines
Reid

Macclesfield Town 1 (AET)
Evans

A late Lee Bowyer header and extra-time goals from Carlton Cole, Zavon Hines and Kyel Reid spared West Ham United's blushes against League Two Macclesfield Town. Gareth Evans had headed the Silkmen ahead, but the Hammers safely negotiated their way through to the Carling Cup third round.

30 AUGUST 2008 – BARCLAYS PREMIER LEAGUE

West Ham United 4
Davenport
Samba (og)
Bellamy
Cole

Blackburn Rovers 1
Roberts

Calum Davenport and a Christopher Samba own goal put West Ham United 2-0 up before Jason Roberts halved the arrears. Roberts saw his penalty saved by Robert Green before Craig Bellamy and Carlton Cole added two late goals.

SEPTEMBER 2008

13 SEPTEMBER 2008 – BARCLAYS PREMIER LEAGUE

West Bromwich Albion 3	West Ham United 2
Morrison	Noble
Bednar (pen)	Neill
Brunt	

With Kevin Keen in charge and Gianfranco Zola watching on, Mark Noble and Lucas Neill scored to put West Ham United 2-1 up following James Morrison's opener. Roman Bednar's penalty and Chris Brunt's late strike won it for West Bromwich Albion.

20 SEPTEMBER 2008 – BARCLAYS PREMIER LEAGUE

West Ham United 3	Newcastle United 1
Di Michele 2	Owen
Etherington	

Gianfranco Zola's first game in charge saw David Di Michele bag a brace and Matthew Etherington his first goal of the season against Newcastle United. Michael Owen scored a late consolation for the Magpies.

23 SEPTEMBER 2008 – CARLING CUP THIRD ROUND

Watford 1	West Ham United 0
Mullins (og)	

A Hayden Mullins own-goal 20 minutes from time was enough to consign West Ham United to a 1-0 Carling Cup third-round defeat at Coca-Cola Championship side Watford.

27 SEPTEMBER 2008 – BARCLAYS PREMIER LEAGUE

Fulham 1	West Ham United 2
Murphy (pen)	Cole
	Etherington

West Ham United made it two Premier League wins out of two under Gianfranco Zola with a thrilling win at ten-man Fulham. The Hammers scored twice just before half-time through Carlton Cole and Matthew Etherington before Andrew Johnson was sent-off. Danny Murphy scored a penalty for the Cottagers.

OCTOBER 2008

5 OCTOBER 2008 – BARCLAYS PREMIER LEAGUE

West Ham United 1
Cole

Bolton Wanderers 3
Davies
Cahill
Taylor

Two uncharacteristic errors from West Ham United goalkeeper Robert Green handed Bolton Wanderers a surprise 3-1 victory at the Boleyn Ground. Kevin Davies and Gary Cahill benefitted to put Bolton 2-0 up before Carlton Cole headed in for the Hammers. Matt Taylor's 35-yard free-kick settled matters.

19 OCTOBER 2008 – BARCLAYS PREMIER LEAGUE

Hull City 1
Turner

West Ham United 0

Barclays Premier League surprise packages Hull City moved into third place in the table with a 1-0 victory over West Ham United at the KC Stadium. Central defender Michael Turner scored the only goal of the game six minutes after half-time, heading in Andy Dawson's corner.

26 OCTOBER 2008 – BARCLAYS PREMIER LEAGUE

West Ham United 0

Arsenal 2
Faubert (og)
Adebayor

West Ham United fell to a third consecutive Barclays Premier League defeat as Arsenal scored twice in the final 15 minutes to leave the Boleyn Ground with all three points. A Julien Faubert own-goal and late Emmanuel Adebayor shot were the difference between the two teams before Carlton Cole was sent off. Michael Turner scored the only goal of the game six minutes after half-time, heading in Andy Dawson's corner.

29 OCTOBER 2008 – BARCLAYS PREMIER LEAGUE

Manchester United 2
Ronaldo 2

West Ham United 0

A first-half brace from Cristiano Ronaldo helped Manchester United to a comfortable victory over West Ham United at Old Trafford. Ronaldo netted Nani's neat cutback before Dimitar Berbatov's breathtaking piece of skill set up the Portuguese forward's second goal heading in Andy Dawson's corner.

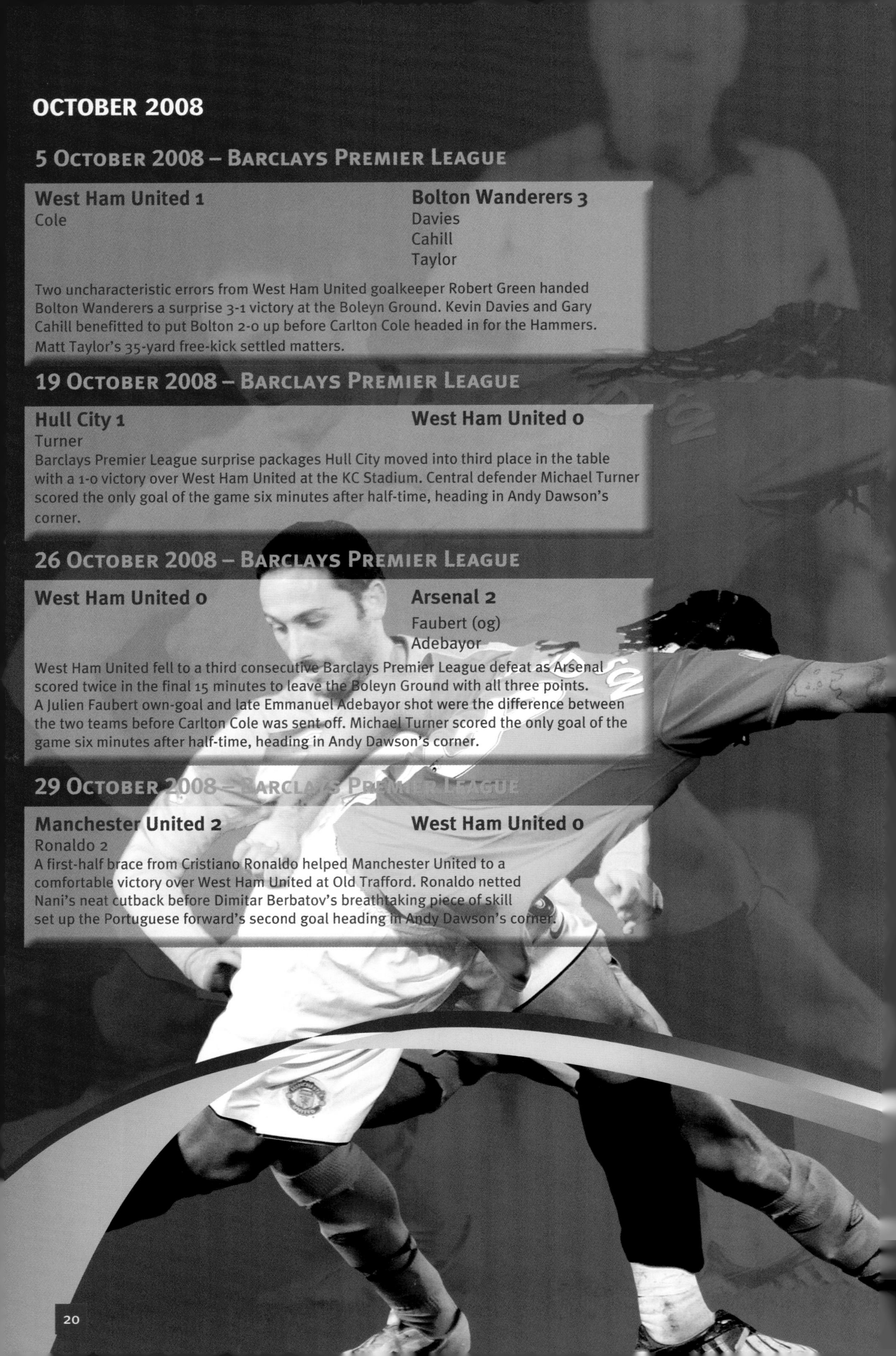

NOVEMBER 2008

1 NOVEMBER 2008 – BARCLAYS PREMIER LEAGUE

Middlesbrough 1
Mido

West Ham United 1
Mullins

A spectacular late double save from Middlesbrough goalkeeper Ross Turnbull prevented West Ham United from leaving Teesside with three deserved points. Earlier, Hayden Mullins had belted in the opening goal before Mido equalised with a powerful low free-kick.

8 NOVEMBER 2008 – BARCLAYS PREMIER LEAGUE

West Ham United 1
Collison

Everton 3
Lescott
Saha 2

Jack Collison's first goal for West Ham United on his home debut was not enough to prevent Everton from storming back to snatch a 3-1 Barclays Premier League victory at the Boleyn Ground. Joleon Lescott and Louis Saha, twice, scored in the final seven minutes for the Toffees.

15 NOVEMBER 2008 – BARCLAYS PREMIER LEAGUE

West Ham United 0

Portsmouth 0

Robert Green kept his first clean-sheet of the season as West Ham United played out a largely uneventful goalless Barclays Premier League draw with Portsmouth at the Boleyn Ground. Ex-Hammer Jermain Defoe missed a host of chances for Pompey.

23 NOVEMBER 2008 – BARCLAYS PREMIER LEAGUE

Sunderland 0

West Ham United 1
Behrami

Valon Behrami scored his first goal for the club as West Ham United ended their seven-match winless run with a Barclays Premier League victory at Sunderland. The Switzerland midfielder was on hand to smash a low shot past Marton Fulop after the Black Cats had failed to clear a 20th minute corner.

DECEMBER 2008

1 DECEMBER 2008 – BARCLAYS PREMIER LEAGUE

Liverpool 0 | West Ham United 0

Buoyed by their victory at Sunderland the previous weekend, West Ham United secured a hard-earned point at Liverpool on Monday 1 December. A superb Robert Green save to deny former team-mate Yossi Benayoun and a long-range Craig Bellamy shot that hit the post were the highlights.

8 DECEMBER 2008 – BARCLAYS PREMIER LEAGUE

West Ham United 0 | Tottenham Hotspur 2
King
O'Hara

West Ham United endured one of their most frustrating 90 minutes of the season as second-half goals from Ledley King and Jamie O'Hara saw Tottenham Hotspur leave the Boleyn Ground with a deserved victory.

14 DECEMBER 2008 – BARCLAYS PREMIER LEAGUE

Chelsea 1 | West Ham United 1
Anelka | Bellamy

West Ham United shrugged off the disappointment of their defeat by Tottenham Hotspur to earn a fully-deserved point at Chelsea five days later. Craig Bellamy shot the Hammers into the lead on 33 minutes following fine play from Mark Noble before Nicolas Anelka levelled for the Blues six minutes after half-time.

20 DECEMBER 2008 – BARCLAYS PREMIER LEAGUE

West Ham United 0 | Aston Villa 1
Neill (og)

Lucas Neill's unfortunate own-goal saw West Ham United fall to a barely-deserved home defeat to Aston Villa. The Hammers had dominated for long periods and could easily have scored before James Milner's cross hit Neill and looped over the helpless Robert Green. Defeat left West Ham 17th in the table after 18 matches.

26 DECEMBER 2008 – BARCLAYS PREMIER LEAGUE

Portsmouth 1 | West Ham United 4
Belhadj | Collison
| Cole
| Bellamy 2

West Ham United celebrated Christmas a day late with a resounding 4-1 Barclays Premier League victory at Portsmouth. Nadir Belhadj opened the scoring for the hosts before Jack Collison, Carlton Cole and Craig Bellamy, twice, hit the target to secure three important points for the Hammers.

28 DECEMBER 2008 – BARCLAYS PREMIER LEAGUE

West Ham United 2 | Stoke City 1
Cole | Abdoulaye Faye
Tristan

West Ham United ended 2008 on a high note by beating ten-man Stoke City thanks to a last-gasp goal from Diego Tristan. Abdoulaye Faye had given the 2007/08 Coca-Cola Championship play-off winners the lead, only for Carlton Cole to equalise, Ricardo Fuller to be sent-off for the Potters and Tristan to glance Cole's shot past Thomas Sorensen for a late winner.

JANUARY 2009

3 JANUARY 2009 – FA CUP THIRD ROUND

West Ham United 3
Ilunga
Noble (pen)
Cole

Barnsley 0

Herita Ilunga's first goal for West Ham United put the Hammers on course for a comfortable FA Cup third-round victory over Coca-Cola Championship outfit Barnsley. Mark Noble's penalty and Carlton Cole's goal completed a fine workout for Gianfranco Zola's side.

10 JANUARY 2009 – BARCLAYS PREMIER LEAGUE

Newcastle United 2
Owen
Carroll

West Ham United 2
Bellamy
Cole

The 300th Barclays Premier League game played at St James' Park ended in an enthralling 2-2 draw, leaving West Ham United tenth in the table. Michael Owen scored early on, only for ex-Magpie Craig Bellamy to equalise. Carlton Cole's vicious volley put West Ham 2-1 up before Anthony Carroll headed in a late leveller.

18 JANUARY 2009 – BARCLAYS PREMIER LEAGUE

West Ham United 3
Di Michele
Noble (pen)
Cole

Fulham 1
Konchesky

Carlton Cole's fifth goal in as many games saw West Ham United complete their first Barclays Premier League double of the season with a 3-1 home win over Fulham. David Di Michele and another Mark Noble penalty completed the victory after former Hammer Paul Konchesky had belted in a stunning long-range equaliser.

24 JANUARY 2009 – FA CUP FOURTH ROUND

Hartlepool United 0

West Ham United 2
Behrami
Noble (pen)

West Ham United avoided a potential FA Cup fourth-round upset with a professional 2-0 victory at Coca-Cola League One side Hartlepool United. Valon Behrami's left-foot shot and yet another Mark Noble penalty saw the Hammers escape the noose at the home of the Monkey Hangers.

28 JANUARY 2009 – BARCLAYS PREMIER LEAGUE

West Ham United 2
Di Michele
Cole

Hull City 0

West Ham United put together one of their best performances of the season in sweeping aside Hull City at the Boleyn Ground. Goals from David Di Michele and Carlton Cole meant Mark Noble's missed penalty, saved by Tigers goalkeeper Matt Duke, did not matter.

31 JANUARY 2009 – BARCLAYS PREMIER LEAGUE

Arsenal 0

West Ham United 0

West Ham United completed an unbeaten January and extended their unbeaten record to eight matches in all competitions with a resilient performance at Arsenal. Central defenders Matthew Upson and James Collins were in particularly impressive form at the Emirates Stadium.

FEBRUARY 2009

8 FEBRUARY 2009 – BARCLAYS PREMIER LEAGUE

West Ham United 0

Manchester United 1
Giggs

A superb individual goal from veteran Manchester United winger Ryan Giggs was the only difference between the two sides as West Ham United's unbeaten run was ended at the Boleyn Ground. The 2008/09 PFA Player of the Year cut inside two challenges before curling a low shot past Robert Green.

14 FEBRUARY 2009 – FA CUP FIFTH ROUND

West Ham United 1
Ilunga

Middlesbrough 1
Downing

Herita Ilunga's late header saved West Ham United from an FA Cup fifth-round exit at the hands of Barclays Premier League strugglers Middlesbrough. The DR Congo left-back's header saved the Hammers' blushes after Stewart Downing had given Boro an early lead.

21 FEBRUARY 2009 – BARCLAYS PREMIER LEAGUE

Bolton Wanderers 2
Taylor
Davies

West Ham United 1
Parker

West Ham United's winless run at the Reebok Stadium was extended to nine matches as the Hammers ran out 2-1 losers at Bolton Wanderers. The Trotters took an early two-goal lead through a Matt Taylor free-kick and Kevin Davies, meaning Scott Parker's second-half strike was nothing more than a consolation.

25 FEBRUARY 2009 – FA CUP FIFTH ROUND REPLAY

Middlesbrough 2
Downing
Tuncay

West Ham United 0

West Ham United plunged out of the FA Cup with a disappointing 2-0 fifth-round replay defeat at Middlesbrough. Stewart Downing's stunning free-kick and Sanli Tuncay's volley were enough to secure victory for the Teessiders.

MARCH 2009

1 MARCH 2009 – BARCLAYS PREMIER LEAGUE

West Ham United 1   **Manchester City 0**
Collison

A superb opportunist volley from Jack Collison saw West Ham United return to winning ways, putting an end to the club's four-match winless run that had spanned the month of February. Earlier, Robert Green had made a fantastic save from Robinho on an afternoon marred by Valon Behrami's serious knee injury.

4 MARCH 2009 – BARCLAYS PREMIER LEAGUE

Wigan Athletic 0   **West Ham United 1**
                                              Cole

Carlton Cole endured a rollercoaster night at the JJB Stadium, scoring West Ham United's goal of the season before being harshly sent-off by referee Stuart Attwell. Cole finished a fine one-touch move involving David Di Michele and Mark Noble before being red carded for an innocuous-looking challenge on Emmerson Boyce.

16 MARCH 2009 – BARCLAYS PREMIER LEAGUE

West Ham United 0   **West Bromwich Albion 0**

After a free weekend following their FA Cup elimination, West Ham United returned to the Boleyn Ground to host relegation-threatened West Bromwich Albion. The Baggies could even have stolen a victory had Robert Green not denied James Morrison and Shelton Martis' header not hit the crossbar.

21 MARCH 2009 – BARCLAYS PREMIER LEAGUE

Blackburn Rovers 1   **West Ham United 1**
Andrews   Noble

Gianfranco Zola's injury-depleted squad showed all their powers of determination in gaining a battling 1-1 draw at Blackburn Rovers. Mark Noble curled in a fine opener from Diego Tristan's pass, only for Keith Andrews to drive in a low shot shortly after half-time to ensure a share of the spoils.

APRIL 2009

4 APRIL 2009 – BARCLAYS PREMIER LEAGUE

West Ham United 2
Stanislas
Tomkins

Sunderland 0

Academy graduates Junior Stanislas and James Tomkins both scored their first senior West Ham United goals as Sunderland were swept aside at the Boleyn Ground. Winger Stanislas slotted in from close-range from Luis Boa Morte's pass before Tomkins rose highest to head Mark Noble's corner past Craig Gordon.

11 APRIL 2009 – BARCLAYS PREMIER LEAGUE

Tottenham Hotspur 1
Pavlyuchenko

West Ham United 0

West Ham United's five-match unbeaten run came to an end with a disappointing 1-0 defeat by Tottenham Hotspur at White Hart Lane. Roman Pavlyuchenko's neat turn and shot with 25 minutes remaining was the only difference between the two sides in north London.

18 APRIL 2009 – BARCLAYS PREMIER LEAGUE

Aston Villa 1
Heskey

West Ham United 1
Tristan

Diego Tristan's superb late header secured West Ham United a share of the spoils as Kieron Dyer made a successful comeback at Aston Villa. The Spaniard diverted Dyer's shot past Brad Friedel after Emile Heskey had given the home side an early lead and later hit a post.

25 APRIL 2009 – BARCLAYS PREMIER LEAGUE

West Ham United 0

Chelsea 1
Kalou

Petr Cech pulled off a fantastic penalty save from Mark Noble as Chelsea beat West Ham United 1-0 at the Boleyn Ground. Salomon Kalou scored the only goal of the game ten minutes after half-time, heading Frank Lampard's cross past Robert Green.

MAY 2009

2 MAY 2009 – BARCLAYS PREMIER LEAGUE

Stoke City 0

West Ham United 1
Tristan

Diego Tristan's inch-perfect free-kick saw West Ham United become just the fourth team to leave Stoke City's Britannia Stadium with a victory during the 2008/09 season. The Spaniard strode up to curl an unstoppable shot past Thomas Sorensen from 25 yards.

9 MAY 2009 – BARCLAYS PREMIER LEAGUE

West Ham United 0

Liverpool 3
Gerrard 2
Babel

An early Steven Gerrard goal put Liverpool on course for a comfortable 3-0 victory at the Boleyn Ground in West Ham United's penultimate home Barclays Premier League fixture. Gerrard added a second after Robert Green had saved his initial penalty before Ryan Babel slotted in a late third from close-range.

16 MAY 2009 – BARCLAYS PREMIER LEAGUE

Everton 3
Saha 2 (1 pen)
Yobo

West Ham United 1
Kovac

Radoslav Kovac's stunning 35-yard screamer appeared to have re-ignited West Ham United's bid for a place in the 2009/10 UEFA Europa League, only for James Tomkins' sending-off to scupper the Hammers' hopes. Louis Saha netted a penalty before Joseph Yobo and another Saha strike put the game beyond West Ham.

24 MAY 2009 – BARCLAYS PREMIER LEAGUE

West Ham United 2
Cole
Stanislas

Middlesbrough 1
O'Neil

West Ham United ended the Barclays Premier League season on a high as relegated Middlesbrough were condemned to a 2-1 defeat at the Boleyn Ground. Carlton Cole, back after a groin injury, put the hosts ahead before Gary O'Neil equalised five minutes after half-time. Junior Stanislas condemned Boro to the drop with a low shot that squeezed past Brad Jones.

HAMMERS QUIZ

1 What was the name of the club before it became West Ham United in July 1900?

2 Who was West Ham United's first manager?

3 In which year were West Ham United elected to the Football League?

4 What was the name of the famous 'White Horse' who helped to control the crowds when West Ham United took on Bolton Wanderers in the 1923 FA Cup final at Wembley?

5 What was the name of the prolific striker who scored an amazing 326 goals in 505 matches for West Ham United between September 1920 and March 1935, making him the club's all-time leading scorer?

6 Which West Ham United legend made his first-team debut in the 3-2 home victory over Manchester United on 8 September 1958?

7 Who scored West Ham United's goals in the 3-2 1964 FA Cup final victory over Preston North End at Wembley?

8 Which German team did West Ham United beat to lift the UEFA Cup Winners' Cup at Wembley in May 1965?

9 Which three West Ham United players were in the England team that lifted the 1966 FIFA World Cup?

10 Who scored both of West Ham United's goals in the 2-0 1975 FA Cup final victory over Fulham?

Answers on page 60

JUBILATION – DANNY GABBIDON CELEBRATES WITH JAMES TOMKINS, CARLTON COLE, JUNIOR STANISLAS AND ZAVON HINES AFTER PUTTING WEST HAM UNITED 1-0 UP IN THE BARCLAYS ASIA TROPHY FIXTURE AGAINST BEIJING GUOAN AT THE WORKERS' STADIUM IN JULY 2009

SUMMER SIGNINGS

Luis Jimenez, Frank Nouble, Fabio Daprela and Jack Lampe all arrived at West Ham United during the summer of 2009.

LUIS JIMENEZ

Born: 17 June 1984, Santiago, Chile
Former clubs: Palestino, Ternana Calcio, ACF Fiorentina, SS Lazio, Internazionale (loan), Internazionale
International caps: Chile
Honours: Chilean Footballer of the Year (2005/06), Serie A winner (2008/09)

Nicknamed 'El Mago' – The Wizard – in his homeland of Chile, Luis Jimenez is widely renowned as one of the most exciting talents in South American football.

Blessed with the ability to beat players with ease, Jimenez – full-name Luis Antonio Jimenez Garces – joined West Ham United on a season-long loan from Italian Serie A champions Internazionale on 23 June 2009.

Jimenez started out with Palestino in his homeland before moving to Italian club Ternana Calcio in 2004. After appearing for Chile at the 2004 Copa America and being named Chile's Player of the year for 2005/06, he enjoyed spells at Fiorentina, Lazio and Inter before moving to London.

FRANK NOUBLE

Born: 24 September 1991, Lewisham, England
Former clubs: Chelsea
International caps: England U17
Honours: None

A powerful and speedy striker, Frank Nouble moved across London from Chelsea to West Ham United on a five-year contract for an undisclosed fee on 21 July 2009.

The top scorer in Chelsea's FA Premier Academy team in 2008/09 with 12 goals, Nouble joined the Blues at the age of eleven. However, he has decided that his long-term future would be better served at the Boley Ground.

A former England Under-17 international, Nouble also appeared in ten Barclays Premier Reserve League So matches last season, scoring twice, and ended the campaign training alongside Didier Drogba and Nico Anelka with the Chelsea first-team squad.

FABIO DAPRELA
Born: 19 February 1991, Zurich, Switzerland
Former clubs: Grasshopper Club Zurich
International caps: Switzerland U17, U19
Honours: None

Switzerland Under-19 defender Fabio Daprela joined West Ham United from Grasshopper Club on 30 July 2009.

Daprela, a highly-rated left-back, flew straight to London to complete his move to the Boleyn Ground from the UEFA European U19 Championship finals in Ukraine. The youngster signed a long-term deal after moving to West Ham from the Zurich club for an undisclosed fee.

Daprela has been a regular for his nation in previous years, starting all three of Switzerland's matches at the 2008 UEFA European U17 Championship finals and the 2009 UEFA U19 Championship finals.

JACK LAMPE
Born: 24 February 1992, Cheshunt, England
Former clubs: Harlow Town
International caps: None
Honours: None

A talented young central defender, Jack Lampe was snapped up from Ryman League club Harlow Town in July 2009 after impressing during a trial at West Ham United.

The tall and powerful 17-year-old appeared in the FA Premier Academy League victory over Fulham at Little Heath in April 2009, showing his potential to Academy Director Tony Carr.

The grandson of former Fulham and England youth international defender Derek Lampe, young Jack names his grandfather and former Hammers Rio Ferdinand and John Terry as his football heroes.

AUSTRIAN ADVENTURE

West Ham United held their pre-season training camp in the idyllic Austrian countryside in preparation for the 2009/10 season, but the pretty surroundings merely provided the backdrop for ten days of intense hard work.

Manager Gianfranco Zola and his coaching staff put the players through their paces in temperatures in excess of 90 degrees at the camp, which was held in the picturesque village of Bad Radkersburg.

Youngsters Anthony Edgar, Olly Lee and Georg Grasser – born just a short distance away in the city of Graz – joined the senior players at the camp. New signing Luis Jimenez also joined his team-mates for the first time following his loan switch from Italian champions Internazionale.

Zola, first-team coaches Steve Clarke and Kevin Keen, goalkeeper coach Ludek Miklosko, reserve team manager Alex Dyer and fitness coach Antonio Pintus were all kept busy as the players enjoyed double training sessions.

While the camp was based on ensuring the players were in peak condition ahead of the new season, the group also found time for some fun and games, riding bikes to and from training and enjoying table tennis and go-karting.

Aside from the training, the Hammers were also scheduled to take part in four pre-season friendlies, only for their prestigious fixture against German Cup winners and UEFA Cup finalists Werder Bremen to be postponed after heavy rainfall left the pitch at Bad Waltersdorf waterlogged.

Three other fixtures were played, however, with West Ham kicking off their tour with a 1-1 draw with Austrian Division Three side SVL Flavia Solva at the Roman Stadium in Wagna. Jack Collison scored the tourists' goal from the penalty spot, while the home side's goal came from Mario Ploschnik.

The second match also ended 1-1, with the Hammers being held by Turkish Super Lig team Bursaspor at the Thermenarena in Bad Radkersburg. Kieron Dyer registered his first goal for the club after three minutes, only for the Turks to equalise through Turgay Bahadir.

West Ham closed their tour with a goalless draw with Slovenian Second Football League outfit ND Mura 05 in Murska Sobota, a short drive over the border in Slovenia.

EIGHT CLASSIC MATCHES

West Ham United 10-0 Bury
League Cup second round second leg
25 October 1983

Four goals from Tony Cottee and a brace apiece from Trevor Brooking and Alan Devonshire helped West Ham United to complete their club record victory against Division Four side Bury. Alvin Martin and Ray Stewart were also on target for the Hammers, but it might have all been so different had Bury's John Bramhall not hit the post with a fourth-minute penalty.

West Ham United 2-1 Tottenham Hotspur
Barclays Premier League
7 May 2006

Tottenham Hotspur asked the Premier League for the match to be put back 24 hours after arriving at the Boleyn Ground with many of their players struck down with a mystery stomach bug. The request was turned down and, with Spurs needing a win to secure a UEFA Champions League place, goals from Carl Fletcher and Yossi Benayoun either side of Jermain Defoe's equaliser put paid to the visitors' hopes.

West Ham United 6-1 West Bromwich Albion
Division One
16 April 1965

Striker Brian Dear produced a stunning individual display to score five times within the space of 20 minutes, inspiring the FA Cup holders to a thrashing of West Bromwich Albion at the Boleyn Ground. Martin Peters had given the hosts a 30th minute lead, which Dear doubled a minute before the break. Jeff Astle halved the deficit on the stroke of half-time, only for 21-year-old Dear to go goal-crazy after the interval, scoring after 53, 56, 59 and 64 minutes.

West Ham United 7-0 Gravesend United
Southern League First Division
1 September 1900

After five years as Thames Ironworks FC, West Ham United burst into existence with a thrashing of Southern League rivals Gravesend United at the Memorial Grounds. William Grassam scored four times and James Reid twice, while the Hammers' other goal was scored by Fergus Hunt. West Ham would end their first season in their new guise in sixth place, while Gravesend would resign from the league.

West Ham United 3-1 Den Haag
UEFA Cup Winners' Cup quarter-final
second leg
17 March 1976

West Ham United completed an amazing comeback to reach the semi-finals of the UEFA Cup Winners' Cup, having trailed 4-0 at half-time during the first leg, eventually losing 4-2. Alan Taylor, Frank Lampard and Billy Bonds put West Ham 5-4 up on aggregate by the interval, only for Lex Schoenmaker to set up a grandstand finish by netting shortly before the hour-mark. The Hammers clung on to go through to a last-four clash with Eintracht Frankfurt.

Preston North End 2-3 West Ham United
FA Cup final
Wembley
2 May 1964

Despite allowing Division Two Preston North End 23 shots on goal, West Ham United twice came from behind to lift the FA Cup for the first time in the club's history. Doug Holden put Preston ahead on ten minutes, only for John Sissons to equalise almost immediately. The Lancastrians went back in front through Alex Dawson before a second-half strike from Geoff Hurst and Ronnie Boyce's last-minute goal saw the trophy make its way to east London.

West Ham United 2-1 Wimbledon
FA Carling Premiership
26 March 2000

Paolo Di Canio was at his brilliant best as West Ham United tore Wimbledon to shreds at the Boleyn Ground. The Italian scored the Goal of the Season after nine minutes, acrobatically volleying past Neil Sullivan from the edge of the penalty area. Frederic Kanoute added a second with a fine header before former Hammer Michael Hughes smashed a shot past Craig Forrest from 25 yards.

Derby County 2-5 West Ham United
FA Cup semi-final
Stamford Bridge
24 March 1923

Billy Moore and William Brown both scored twice as West Ham United thrashed fellow Division Two side Derby County to reach the FA Cup final just four years after their election to the Football League. Jimmy Ruffell was also on target as the Hammers swept aside the Rams in front of a 50,795-strong crowd at Chelsea's Stamford Bridge home. West Ham would go on to lose 2-0 to Bolton Wanderers in the first Wembley final the following month.

GIANFRANCO ZOLA FIRST-TEAM MANAGER

Born: 5 July 1966, Oliena, Sardinia, Italy

Playing career: Nuorese (1984-1986), Torres (1986–1989), SSC Napoli (1989–1993), AS Parma (1993–1996), Chelsea (1996–2003), Cagliari (2003–2005), Italy (1991-1997)

Managerial career: Italy Under-21 (assistant coach, 2006-2008), West Ham United (2008-)

One of the finest foreign-born players to grace English football, Gianfranco Zola has made a seamless transition into management at West Ham United. Born in the month West Ham's Bobby Moore, Geoff Hurst and Martin Peters helped England to FIFA World Cup glory, Zola enjoyed a hugely successful playing career with Napoli, Parma, Chelsea, Cagliari and Italy before becoming coach of the Italian Under-21 side and moving on to join the Hammers in September 2008.

STEVE CLARKE FIRST-TEAM COACH

Born: 29 August 1963, Saltcoats, Scotland

Playing career: St Mirren (1982-1987), Chelsea (1987-1998), Scotland (1987-1994)

Managerial career: Newcastle United (caretaker manager, 1999), Chelsea (assistant manager, 2004-2008), West Ham United (2008-)

A consistent full-back for both club and country, former Scotland international Steve Clarke was appointed as West Ham United's first-team coach on 15 September 2008. Clarke got down to work on the same day as ex-Chelsea team-mate and long-time friend Gianfranco Zola. Having enjoyed a successful playing career with St Mirren and Chelsea, Clarke came into his own as a coach under Jose Mourinho at Chelsea before following Zola to east London.

KEVIN KEEN FIRST-TEAM COACH

Born: 25 February 1967, Amersham, England

Playing career: Wycombe Wanderers (1982-83), West Ham United (1983-1993), Wolverhampton Wanderers (1993-1994), Stoke City (1994-2000), Macclesfield Town (2000-2001)

Managerial career: Macclesfield Town (caretaker manager, 2001), West Ham United (caretaker manager, 2006 and 2008)

The son of former Luton Town, Watford and Queens Park Rangers player Mike Keen, Kevin has become an integral part of the coaching staff at West Ham United. A skilfu midfielder in his own playing days, Keen turned out for the Hammers for a decade. Following his retirement, he has fulfilled the role of reserve team and caretaker manager before being appointed as a first-team coach following the arrival of Gianfranco Zola as manager.

LUDEK MIKLOSKO FIRST-TEAM GOALKEEPING COACH

Born: 9 December 1961, Prostejov, Czechoslovakia

Playing career: Union Cheb (1980-82), Banik Ostrava (1982-1990), West Ham United (1990-1998), Queens Park Rangers (1998-2001), Czechoslovakia (1982-1993), Czech Republic (1996-97)

A hugely popular goalkeeper who made 375 first-team appearances for West Ham United, Ludek Miklosko is now the club's first-team goalkeeping coach. 'Ludo' made his name with Banik Ostrava in the country formerly known as Czechoslovakia. After moving to West Ham in 1990, Miklosko quickly established himself and became a fans' favourite. Following his retirement, he returned to the Boleyn Ground as goalkeeping coach.

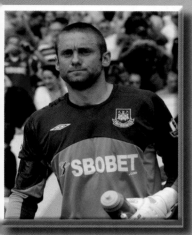

ROBERT GREEN
Goalkeeper
Born: 18 January 1980, Chertsey, England

An England international, Robert Green joined West Ham United from Norwich City in August 2006. A consistent performer, Green started 88 consecutive Barclays Premier League matches up until the end of the 2008/09 season. The goalkeeper played a starring role as West Ham escaped relegation in the Spring of 2007, before being named Hammer of the Year at the end of the following campaign. A popular player, Green made his England debut in the 3-2 friendly win over Colombia in East Rutherford, New Jersey, in May 2005. Off the pitch, Green climbed Mount Kilimanjaro in Tanzania in June 2008 for the charity AMREF (African Medical and Research Foundation).

DANIEL GABBIDON
Defender
Born: 8 August 1979, Cwmbran, Wales

A tenacious competitor, Daniel Gabbidon showed all his determination to return to full training in the summer of 2009 after 18 months out of action with a complicated abdominal problem. Having started his career at West Bromwich Albion, Gabbidon made his name at Cardiff City, being named in the PFA Division One Team of the Season in 2003/04. Gabbidon joined West Ham on the same day as Cardiff and Wales team-mate and close friend James Collins in July 2005. A year later, he was part of the Hammers team narrowly beaten by Liverpool in the FA Cup final at the Millennium Stadium, the same season he was voted as Hammer of the Year by the club's supporters.

MATTHEW UPSON
Defender
Born: 18 April 1979, Hartismere, England

A composed, consistent central defender, Matthew Upson has become an influential figure at the Boleyn Ground since joining West Ham United on the final day of the January transfer window in 2007. Upson has forged a reputation as a calm, assured presence at the heart of the Hammers' rearguard, forcing his way into Fabio Capello's senior England squad in the process. Upson began his career at Luton Town before joining Arsenal as a teenager. There, injuries and competition for places restricted his opportunities. Loan spells at Nottingham Forest, Crystal Palace and Reading followed before the defender joined Birmingham City. His fine form for the Blues persuaded the Hammers to bring him to London.

KIERON DYER
Midfielder
Born: 29 December 1978, Ipswich, England

Kieron Dyer was one of the brightest prospects in English football when he broke through at hometown club Ipswich Town more than a decade ago. That potential has been translated into more than 30 senior England caps and a successful club career. However, injuries have restricted Dyer's appearances since his arrival at West Ham United in the summer of 2007. A broken leg ruled him out for much of the 2007/08 campaign, while the 2008/09 season was also marred by further niggling injury problems. The speedy player scored his first goal for the club during a pre-season friendly against Turkish team Bursaspor in Austria in July 2009.

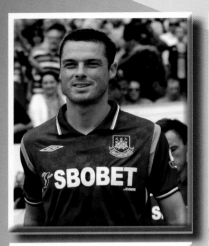

SCOTT PARKER
Midfielder
Born: 13 October 1980, Lambeth, England

An England international, Scott Parker first came to the nation's attention when he appeared juggling a football in McDonald's television adverts during the 1994 FIFA World Cup. From there, Parker established himself in the first-team at Charlton Athletic, catching the eye with his tough tackling and never-say-die attitude. Those qualities saw Jose Mourinho spend £10m to take him across London to Chelsea in January 2004. Parker moved on again 18 months later, joining Newcastle United, where he was later made captain. After winning the UEFA Intertoto Cup in 2006, Parker joined West Ham United in the summer of 2007. A series of whole-hearted displays saw Parker voted Hammer of the Year at the end of the 2008/09 campaign.

DEAN ASHTON
Forward
Born: 24 November 1983, Swindon, England

England striker Dean Ashton burst on to the scene at Crewe Alexandra as a teenager a decade ago. At Gresty Road, under the watchful eye of Dario Gradi, the powerful forward became one of the hottest young properties in the country. Ashton plundered a hatful of goals for the Railwaymen, tempting Norwich City to spend £3m and make the striker their record signing in January 2005. A year later, he was on the move again as West Ham spent £7.25m to bring the England U21 man to the Boleyn Ground. Ashton's goals helped the Hammers reach the 2006 FA Cup final, where he scored against Liverpool. However, a broken ankle suffered in training with England halted his progress in August 2006. Ashton recovered sufficiently to make his full international debut against Trinidad and Tobago on 1 June 2008.

SAVIO
Forward
Born: 27 July 1989, Kampala, Uganda

A Germany Under-20 forward, Savio was born in the Ugandan capital Kampala before his family moved to Munich when he was just two. There, the skilful attacker impressed for TSV 1860 Munich before being spotted by West Ham United technical director Gianluca Nani, who was then fulfilling a similar role for Italian club Brescia Calcio. After three-and-a-half years in Italy, Savio followed Nani to London to join the Hammers, making his debut in the 2-0 Barclays Premier League win over Hull City on 28 January 2009. On the international scene, Savio was an integral part of the Germany squad that lifted the UEFA European U19 Championship trophy in the summer of 2008.

CARLTON COLE
Forward
Born: 12 October 1983, Croydon, England

Under the direction of West Ham United manager Gianfranco Zola and first-team coaches Steve Clarke and Kevin Keen, Carlton Cole emerged as one of the most-feared strikers in the Barclays Premier League. Cole's form in claret and blue during 2008/09 earned the powerful, speedy striker a new five-year contract at the Boleyn Ground as well as a full England debut. A return of 12 goals in all competitions was also a career-high for the Croydon-born player, who has become an influential figure for the Hammers. Cole began his career alongside Zola and Clarke at Chelsea before enjoying loan spells at Wolverhampton Wanderers, Charlton Athletic and Aston Villa.

LUIS BOA MORTE
Midfielder
Born: 4 August 1977, Lisbon, Portugal

A committed, whole-hearted performer, Luis Boa Morte has become an important member of the West Ham United squad since joining the Hammers from Fulham in early January 2007. A Portuguese international, he began his career at Sporting Clube de Portugal - in the city of his birth, Lisbon - before spending a short period on loan at SC Lourinhanense. Boa Morte moved to England in the summer of 1997 after being spotted by Arsenal manager Arsène Wenger at the prestigious Toulon Under-21 Tournament in France. After two years at Highbury, Boa Morte joined Southampton before moving back to London with Fulham, where he became a huge success, helping the Cottagers to lift the Football League Championship trophy in 2001.

MARK NOBLE
Midfielder
Born: 8 May 1987, Canning Town, England

A popular figure with both his West Ham United team-mates and supporters, Mark Noble has come through the ranks to establish himself in the first team and is now the club's longest-serving player. Noble became the youngest player to turn out for the Hammers' reserve team at the age of 15 in February 2003, when coach Roger Cross called his school to ask for the midfielder to be excused from lessons. Four months later, Noble signed his first Academy professional contract. Since then, he has barely looked back, clocking up more than 100 appearances for the first-team and being named as England's captain at the UEFA European Under-21 Championship in the summer of 2009.

LUIS JIMENEZ
Forward
Born: 17 June 1984, Santiago, Chile

Nicknamed 'El Mago' – The Wizard – in his homeland of Chile, Luis Jimenez is widely renowned as one of the most exciting talents in South American football. Blessed with the ability to beat players with ease, Jimenez joined West Ham United on a season-long loan from Italian Serie A champions Internazionale. Prior to his move to London, the Chile international started his career at Palestino in his homeland before moving to Italian club Ternana in 2004. Loan spells at Fiorentina and Lazio followed before Jimenez moved to Internazionale on a permanent basis in the summer of 2008. A tricky and skilful player, Jimenez can play out wide, in the centre of midfield or in a more advanced, attacking role.

JONATHAN SPECTOR
Defender
Born: 1 March 1986, Arlington Heights, USA

The grandson of NBA star Art Spector, the first player to be signed by the Boston Celtics, Jonathan Spector is a versatile member of the West Ham United squad. Comfortable at either full-back or centre-back and more than useful in a defensive midfield role, Spector is a fully committed player who will never shirk a challenge. Possessing a German passport through his grandmother, Spector decided to pursue his dream of becoming a professional in Europe, joining Manchester United in the summer of 2003. After spending a season on loan at Charlton Athletic, Spector would join West Ham in June 2006. At international level, the defender was ever-present as the USA reached the final of the FIFA Confederations Cup in South Africa in the summer of 2009.

PETER KURUCZ
Goalkeeper
Born: 30 May 1988, Budapest, Hungary

Hungary Under-21 goalkeeper Peter Kurucz joined West Ham United on a four-year contract from Ujpest FC in July 2009. Kurucz made nine first-team appearances for Budapest-based Ujpest and also spent a period on loan at FC Tatabanya. Following his arrival on loan in January 2009, he made his competitive debut for West Ham in the 2-0 Barclays Premier Reserve League South defeat by Aston Villa on 17 March 2009. The youngster was an unused substitute in the penultimate Barclays Premier League game of the 2008/09 season away to Everton before joining the first-team squad on their summer training camp in Austria.

JAMES COLLINS
Defender
Born: 23 August 1983, Newport, Wales

A whole-hearted central defender, James Collins has represented his native Wales at every level from Under-15 to the senior side, for whom he has won more than 25 caps since making his debut as a 20-year-old against Norway in 2004. Tipped to reach the highest level from an early age, Collins made his first-team debut for first club Cardiff City at the age of 17 in an FA Cup first-round tie against Bristol Rovers in November 2000. Having impressed for the Bluebirds, Collins joined West Ham United in July 2005 helping the club to reach the FA Cup final in his first season at the Boleyn Ground. Injuries have hindered Collins over the past two years, but he still retains the qualities that have made him a popular figure at the club since his arrival.

JULIEN FAUBERT
Defender
Born: 1 August 1983, Le Havre, France

Julien Faubert rejected the advances of several leading European clubs to cross the Channel to join West Ham United from Bordeaux for a £6.1m fee in July 2007. Born in Le Havre, Faubert headed south in 1998 when he was offered a place at the AS Cannes youth academy, famous for nurturing such talents as Zinedine Zidane, Johan Micoud and Patrick Vieira. From Cannes, Faubert joined Bordeaux, helping the club to finish second in the Ligue Un table in 2005/06. The fast and powerful midfielder scored on his international debut for France against Bosnia-Herzegovina on 16 August 2006, scoring a last-minute winner. Having seen his first season at West Ham disrupted by a ruptured Achilles tendon, Faubert spent the second half of the 2008/09 season on loan at Real Madrid.

VALON BEHRAMI
Midfielder
Born: 19 April 1985, Mitrovica, Kosovo

Born in the town of Mitrovica in what is now Kosovo, the hugely popular Valon Behrami moved with his family to the village of Stabio in Italian-speaking Switzerland as a small child. After playing for local sides FC Stabio and Chiasso, Behrami joined FC Lugano, making his first-team debut for the club in 2002. A year later, he moved across the border to Italy, joining Genoa. A loan spell followed at Hellas Verona before Behrami joined Lazio in 2005. West Ham United snapped up the highly-rated Switzerland international in July 2008, and Behrami enjoyed a superb first season in London. For his adopted country, Behrami has appeared at the 2006 FIFA World Cup and 2008 UEFA European Championship.

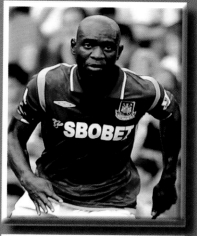

HERITA ILUNGA
Defender
Born: 25 February 1982, Kinshasa, DR Congo

Born in Kinshasa in February 1982, Herita Ilunga moved with his family to Paris as a child, starting his football career in the northern suburb of Sarcelles. At the age of 13, Ilunga started training with Amiens SC, staying with the Somme-based club for four years before moving to Stade Rennais. Ilunga decided to try his luck abroad, joining Espanyol in Barcelona in 2002, before heading back to France and St Etienne a year later. The summer of 2007 saw the left-back move to Toulouse, where he appeared against Liverpool in the UEFA Champions League. A regular member of the DR Congo international squad, Ilunga joined West Ham United on loan in September 2008 before making his move permanent by signing a contract until June 2013.

MAREK STECH
Goalkeeper
Born: 28 January 1990, Prague, Czech Republic

Czech Republic Under-21 international Marek Stech is eager to follow in the giant footsteps of Czech countryman Ludek Miklosko by becoming a hero between the sticks at the Boleyn Ground. Born in Prague in January 1990, Stech began his career with hometown club Sparta Prague as a 12-year-old in 2002. Having come through the ranks with the Czech giants, the young stopper came to the world's attention by helping his country reach the final of the UEFA European Under-17 Championship in 2006. A regular in West Ham United's reserve team, Stech joined League Two promotion-chasers Wycombe Wanderers on loan until the end of the season in March 2009, making two senior appearances.

JAMES TOMKINS
Defender
Born: 29 March 1989, Basildon, England

A central defender mature beyond his years, James Tomkins has settled into life in the Barclays Premier League like a duck to water. Tipped for a bright future in the game since he was a promising youngster, Tomkins has featured for England at every age-group from Under-15 to Under-21, making his bow at the latter level in June 2009. A product of West Ham United's Academy, Tomkins joined the club at the tender age of seven. Tomkins made his West Ham United debut in the 1-1 draw at Everton in March 2008, before going on loan to Championship side Derby County in early 2009 before establishing himself in Gianfranco Zola's side during the second half of the 2008/09 season. Tomkins was also part of England's U21 squad at the 2009 European Championship finals in Sweden.

JACK COLLISON
Midfielder
Born: 2 October 1988, Watford, England

A full Wales international at the age of 19, young midfielder Jack Collison has made huge strides forward since leaving his teenage years behind. Collison began his career with Peterborough United as a youngster before moving to Cambridge United. Collison moved to West Ham United in the summer of 2005, going on to impress and be named captain of the club's reserve team a short time later. After impressing on the Hammers pre-season tour of the USA in 2008, Collison forced his way into Gianfranco Zola's thinking with an impressive display against Manchester United at Old Trafford in October. A first goal arrived on his home debut against Everton as the midfielder ended the season by being voted Young Hammer of the Year.

FREDDIE SEARS
Forward
Born: 27 November 1989, Hornchurch, England

A prolific goalscorer at Under-18 and reserve team level, livewire striker Freddie Sears is eager to join the long line of homegrown West Ham United strikers to make their ma at the highest level. He had scored 25 goals in 24 matches for the youths and reserves during the 2007/08 campaign, and just signed a new deal with the club by the time he made it on to the bench on 15 March for the visit of Blackburn Rovers. He came on with 16 minutes to play and barely five minutes later had headed the winner in a rousing 2-1 home win. Sears found it more difficult to make an impact during the 2008/09 campaign, but still managed all four goals in a reserve team win over West Bromwich Albion. The youngster, an England U20 international, joined Coca-Cola Championship side Crystal Palace on a season-long loan deal in the summer of 2009.

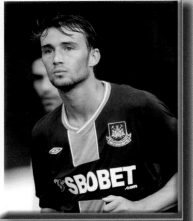

JOSH PAYNE
Midfielder
Born: 25 November 1990, Basingstoke, England

An energetic midfielder and sometime central defender, Josh Payne began the 2008/09 season as West Ham United's Under-18 captain. By the end of it, he was a regular member of Gianfranco Zola's first-team squad. After representing both Portsmouth and Southampton as a youngster, Payne joined West Ham in early 2007, impressing Academy Director Tony Carr with his all-round ability and attitude. Payne's development continued as he became a regular in the reserve side before being promoted to the first-team squad midway through the 2008/09 campaign. A Barclays Premier League debut arrived at Blackburn Rovers at Ewood Park on 21 March 2009. A second appearance came against Liverpool on 9 May.

HOLMAR ORN EYJOLFSSON
Defender
Born: 6 August 1990, Saudarkrokur, Iceland

The son of former Iceland midfielder and coach Eyjolfur Sverrisson, Holmar Orn Eyjolfsson is rated as one of the brightest prospects in Icelandic football. Following a week-long trial in early 2008, the powerful central defender joined West Ham United from HK Kopavogur on a permanent basis on 4 July of the same year, becoming the club's first acquisition of the summer. At international level, Eyjolfsson was capped at U16 and U17 level, being singled out by UEFA as a player to watch for the future at the UEFA European U17 Championship in Belgium in 2007. An U21 debut arrived in November 2007.

ZAVON HINES
Forward
Born: 27 December 1988, Kingston, Jamaica

Zavon Hines is a pacy young forward who developed well in the 2007/08 campaign but really took off in the following season, scoring on his first-team debut against Macclesfield Town in the Carling Cup second round at the Boleyn Ground. Born in December 1988, Hines was involved in pre-season action before starting as a regular in the reserves. In March 2008, Hines was loaned for a month to Coca-Cola Championship club Coventry City. His potential was also recognised with a call-up to the Jamaica squad for the friendly international with Nigeria at Loftus Road in February 2009.

JUNIOR STANISLAS
Midfielder
Born: 26 November 1989, Kidbrooke, England

A lively, tricky, speedy winger, Junior Stanislas has been with West Ham United since the age of ten. After nearly a decade of hard work, Stanislas was handed his Barclays Premier League debut in the goalless draw with West Bromwich Albion at the Boleyn Ground on 16 March 2009. Three weeks later, the wideman was handed his first start in a claret and blue shirt for the visit of Sunderland. Stanislas responded by scoring his first goal for the club in a 2-0 home victory also marked by James Tomkins' maiden goal for the Hammers. An England Under-20 international, Stanislas produced a superb display in his country's friendly victory over Italy at Loftus Road in March 2009.

BONDZ N'GALA
Defender
Born: 13 September 1989, Forest Gate, England

A powerful, aggressive central defender, Bondz N'Gala emerged through the ranks at West Ham United to be named as the club's reserve team captain midway through the 2008/09 season. Increasingly comfortable in possession, N'Gala joined the Hammers as a 13-year-old, impressing Academy coaches with his commitment and willingness to learn. In recent seasons, the defender's game has come on leaps and bounds. Having enjoyed loan spells at Weymouth and MK Dons, N'Gala was named as an unused substitute for West Ham's Barclays Premier League win over Stoke City in December 2008 and joined the first-team on their pre-season training camp in Austria in the summer of 2009.

JORDAN SPENCE
Defender
Born: 24 May 1990, Woodford, England

Jordan Spence has enjoyed a prodigious rise since joining West Ham United in 2004. Already a fixture for England at Under-19 level, Spence is now planning to force his way into Gianfranco Zola's thinking at the Boleyn Ground. Born in Woodford and a former Chigwell School pupil, Spence captained England's U16 side before leading the U17s to the FIFA World Cup in South Korea in 2007. There, he became the first Englishman to score a winner against Brazil in a competitive international as he led his country to the quarter-finals. Spence earned further caps at U19 level, helping England to reach the 2009 European Championship finals. Back at club level, the teenager also enjoyed a successful loan spell at League One Leyton Orient during the 2008/09 campaign.

TERRY DIXON
Forward
Born: 15 January 1990, Archway, England

Rated as one of Irish football's brightest prospects, West Ham United swooped to capture Terry Dixon in February 2009 on a three-year contract. Dixon was capped by the Republic of Ireland at every level up to Under-21 before being named in the senior squad by Steve Staunton for the friendly against Chile in May 2006 at the tender age of 16. Then with Tottenham Hotspur, Ireland's U17 Player of the Year for 2006 was struck down by a serious knee injury and released by Spurs in March 2008.

SPOT THE DIFFERENCE

Can you find the 6 differences between these two pictures?

ANSWERS ON PAGE 60

MATTHEW UPSON

TEN THINGS YOU NEVER KNEW ABOUT WEST HAM UNITED

1 West Ham United's previous home at the Memorial Grounds in Canning Town was said to have an estimated maximum capacity of 120,000.

2 HM King Olav V of Norway visited the Boleyn Ground for West Ham United's 2-1 Division One defeat by Sheffield United on 6 November 1971.

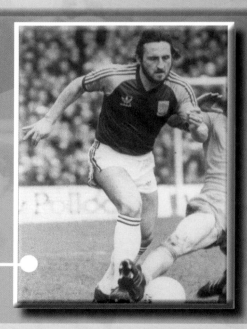

3 Four sets of fathers and sons have played for West Ham United, all of whom shared common forenames – Jim Barrett Sr and Jim Barrett Jr, Bill Lansdowne Sr and Billy Lansdowne, Ken Brown and Kenny Brown and Frank Lampard Sr And Frank Lampard Jr.

4 West Ham United went on their first foreign tour in 1921, visiting Spain where they beat Madrid 4-0, Vigo 4-0, Bilbao 2-0 and Corunna 1-0.

5 The first match played under floodlights at the Boleyn Ground took place on 16 April 1953. West Ham United beat Tottenham Hotspur 2-1.

6 West Ham United lost just one home league game during the 1980/81 season, which saw the club crowned as Division Two champions. Luton Town were the only visitors to leave with maximum points, winning the opening match of the season 2-1 on 16 August 1980.

7 West Ham United are the only club to win two FA Cup finals with all-English teams, having done so in 1964 and 1975.

1963-64

8 West Ham United's Division One fixture with Manchester United on 16 May 1977 was the first all-ticket match at the Boleyn Ground after the Second World War. West Ham won 4-2.

9 West Ham United and Wales inside-forward Phil Woosnam took temporary charge of the first-team between the resignation of Ted Fenton and the appointment of Ron Greenwood in 1961. Woosnam was just 28 at the time.

10 Only one player whose surname begins with the letter 'Z' has ever played for West Ham United. Striker Bobby Zamora scored 40 goals in 152 games between February 2004 and May 2008.

TONY CARR
ACADEMY DIRECTOR

Tony Carr is quite simply one of the best Academy Directors on the planet. Since joining the West Ham United Academy in 1973, he has overseen the development of countless youngsters who have gone on to play at the very highest level.

A player himself in his youth, Carr was on West Ham's books during the mid-1960s, when he cleaned the boots of England's FIFA World Cup-winning striker Geoff Hurst at Chadwell Heath. An injury curtailed his own hopes of forging a successful playing career, so he instead turned to coaching. It turned out to be an inspired choice.

After initially starting out as a part-time assistant coach in 1973 at the request of assistant manager John Lyall, Carr was promoted to the role of Academy Director and well on the way to relishing the opportunity to put his own stamp on the famous Academy.

From Ron Greenwood to Gianfranco Zola, manager after manager at the Boleyn Ground has felt the benefit of Carr's unstinting commitment to excellence and developing the stars of tomorrow. The Academy Director's aim has always been to produce well-rounded individuals who understand every aspect of the 'West Ham way'.

A host of future internationals have come through the ranks at Little Heath, all of them having benefited from Carr's expert tutelage, having initially been spotted by members of the club's peerless scouting network.

England internationals Alvin Martin, Tony Cottee, Paul Ince, Frank Lampard, Rio Ferdinand, Joe Cole, Michael Carrick, Glen Johnson, Jermain Defoe, Kieran Richardson and John Terry, Republic of Ireland star Ray Houghton, Wales internationals Freddy Eastwood and Jack Collison, Northern Ireland player Grant McCann and Australian internationals Richard Garcia and Chris Coyne have all emerged from the Academy during Carr's reign.

Alongside them, countless top-flight players have also graduated from the Academy, including Bobby Barnes, Mervyn Day, Alan Dickens, Paul Brush, Paul Allen, Geoff Pike, George Parris, Steve Potts, Kevin Keen, Stuart Slater, Danny Williamson, Elliott Ward, Jlloyd Samuel, Liam Ridgewell and Anton Ferdinand, as well as present-day stars such as England Under-21 captain Mark Noble, James Tomkins, Junior Stanislas, Josh Payne and Freddie Sears.

In short, Carr's contribution to West Ham United has been unrivalled in the modern history of the club and, perhaps, English football as a whole.

In March 2009 it was announced that in recognition of Carr's 36 years of service to West Ham he had been awarded a testimonial by the club.

FANS

TEN HAMMERS GREATS

BOBBY MOORE OBE (1958-1974)
Appearances: 646
Goals: 27

Imperious, composed and unflappable, Bobby Moore was quite simply one of the finest footballers the world has ever seen. Capped 108 times by England, who he captained to FIFA World Cup triumph in 1966, Moore is a true West Ham United legend. After making his debut at 17 in 1958, central defender Moore captained the Hammers to FA Cup glory in 1964 and the UEFA Cup Winners' Cup a year later. In 1966, Moore was back at Wembley to lift the FIFA World Cup for England.

Made an OBE in January 1967, Moore starred again at the 1970 World Cup. In total, he made 646 appearances for West Ham, playing his final game in January 1974. Four times Hammer of the Year, Moore was back at Wembley in 1975 as part of the Fulham team beaten 2-0 by the Hammers in the FA Cup final. Moore passed away following a battle with cancer in February 1993. He was just 51.

VIC WATSON (1920-1935)
Appearances: 505
Goals: 326

Put simply and in modern-day parlance, Vic Watson was a 'Goal Machine'. Born in the Cambridgeshire village of Girton on 10 November 1897, West Ham United's all-time leading scorer notched up an amazing 326 goals in 505 appearances for the club.

After starting his career with local club Girton, Watson represented Cambridge Town, Peterborough and Fletton United and Brotherhood Engineering Works before joining West Ham in March 1920. Over the next 15 years, his record would be nothing short of phenomenal.

On nine occasions, Watson scored 20 or more league goals in a season. On 9 February 1929, he plundered six goals in an 8-2 Division One win over Leeds United at the Boleyn Ground. The following season, 1929/30, Watson notched 42 league goals and 50 in total – both club records. Watson, who earned five England caps, died in 1988 at the age of 90.

SIR TREVOR BROOKING CBE (1967-1984)
Appearances: 635
Goals: 102

A true 'one-club man', Trevor Brooking signed for West Ham United as an apprentice in July 1965, playing his final first-team game for the club nearly 19 years later in May 1984. A modern midfield player, Brooking was born in Barking on 2 October 1948, joining the club straight from Ilford County High School. He made his senior debut for the Hammers in a 3-3 Division One draw at Burnley on 29 August 1967. It would be the first of 635 first-team appearances for the club.

Brooking's most famous moment in a West Ham shirt came on 10 May 1980, when he stooped to head the only goal of the game as Arsenal were beaten 1-0 in the FA Cup final at Wembley. He had also won a winner's medal in 1975.

At international level, Brooking won 47 caps for England, scoring five goals and appearing at the 1982 FIFA World Cup in Spain. He returned to the Boleyn Ground in 2003 as caretaker manager, losing just one of his 14 matches in charge.

SIR GEOFF HURST MBE (1958-1972)
Appearances: 502
Goals: 252

What many West Ham United supporters are blissfully unaware of is the fact that, had it not been for a masterstroke by Hammers manager Ron Greenwood, England's 1966 FIFA World Cup hero may never have become a striker. Geoff Hurst spent the early part of his career as a wing-half, only reverting to a more advanced role when Greenwood identified his qualities as fitting those of a forward.

The son of professional footballer Charlie Hurst, Geoff was born in Ashton-under-Lyne, Lancashire, on 8 December 1941. Having moved south when his father joined Chelmsford City, Hurst made his first-team debut as a 17-year-old.

Hurst won both the FA Cup and UEFA Cup Winners' Cup before returning to Wembley to net a 'perfect' hat-trick in the 4-2 1966 FIFA World Cup final win over West Germany.

In total, Hurst plundered 252 goals in 502 games for West Ham, notching a further 24 in 49 appearances for his country. He was made an MBE in 1975 and knighted in 1998.

TONY COTTEE (1983-1988 / 1994-1996)
Appearances: 336
Goals: 146

Few West Ham United players have burst on to the scene in quite the same way Tony Cottee did. On New Year's Day 1983, at the age of 17, Cottee marked his first-team debut with the opening goal in a 3-0 win over arch-rivals Tottenham Hotspur at the Boleyn Ground. A legend had been born.

Cottee would go on to score 146 goals in 336 games for the Hammers, forging a feared partnership with Scot Frank McAvennie. The pair combined to net 46 First Division goals in season 1985/86, leading West Ham to their highest-ever league placing of third.

Born in Plaistow on 11 July 1965, Cottee scored four goals in the 10-0 League Cup victory over Bury in October 1983 and was voted PFA Young Player of the Year in 1986. He also earned seven England caps.

JIM BARRETT SR (1925-1945)
Appearances: 467
Goals: 53

A powerfully-built centre-half, Jim Barrett was one of West Ham United's most important players in the period between the two World Wars. Born in Stratford on 19 January 1907, Barrett initially attended the Abbey School before moving to the nearby Park School because the former did not have a football team.

Barrett plundered more than 200 goals for Park before joining the famous Fairbairn House Boys' Club and signing professional terms with West Ham in 1923. After making his debut in March 1925, he would go on to make 467 appearances and score 53 goals for the club. He also earned one England cap in October 1928.

Following his retirement, Barrett took charge of the club's junior teams, overseeing the emergence of son Jim Jr, who scored 25 goals in 87 games for West Ham between April 1950 and December 1954.

BILLY BONDS MBE (1967-1988)
Appearances: 793
Goals: 59

A true West Ham United legend, Billy Bonds spent 21 years in the first-team, winning two FA Cup winner's medals and being voted Hammer of the Year on four occasions.

Born just over the River Thames in Woolwich on 17 September 1946, Bonds joined local club Charlton Athletic at the age of 15 before being tempted to the Boleyn Ground by Ron Greenwood in May 1967. Bonds became a stalwart at the heart of the West Ham side, whether it was in the centre of defence or midfield. In total, he would make 793 first-team appearances for the Hammers – well over 100 more than any other player in the club's long history.

In 1975, Bonds captained West Ham to FA Cup glory against Fulham at Wembley, repeating the trick against Arsenal five years later. Following his retirement, Bonds was made an MBE in 1988, becoming a youth coach under John Lyall before taking over as manager in February 1990, leading the club to promotion to Division One in 1990/91 and 1992/93.

PHIL PARKES (1979-1990)
Appearances: 444
Goals: 0

A hugely popular figure, goalkeeper Phil Parkes made 444 first-team appearances during his eleven-year stay with West Ham United. Born in Sedgley, Staffordshire, on 8 August 1950 he joined Walsall as a teenager.

After starting his career with the Sadlers, Parkes joined Queens Park Rangers in 1970, spending nine years with the club and making 406 first-team appearances. Parkes moved across London to West Ham in February 1979, joining the Hammers for a fee of £565,000, a world record fee for a goalkeeper at the time. He would quickly justify the outlay and establish himself as the club's No1, playing his part in the club's FA Cup final win over Arsenal in 1980. A year later, he was named Hammer of the Year.

Capped once by England, Parkes was voted as the goalkeeper in West Ham's greatest-ever team.

JIMMY RUFFELL (1921-1937)
Appearances: 548
Goals: 166

Although he was born in the Yorkshire town of Doncaster on 8 August 1900, Jimmy Ruffell quickly became an adopted Londoner during his 17-year career with West Ham United. After an early career that included stops at Fullers FC, Chadwell Heath United, Manor Park Albion, East Ham and Wall End United, Ruffell joined West Ham United in March 1920.

Ruffell would make 548 appearances in a West Ham shirt, scoring 166 goals. While he regularly found the net himself, Ruffell also supplied countless crosses for the club's greatest goal-scorer Vic Watson. The wideman's efforts earned him six England caps, all of which came against the home nations between April 1926 and November 1929.

Having picked up an FA Cup runners-up medal in 1923, Ruffell left West Ham in 1937, joining Aldershot before retiring from the game. He died on 6 September 1989 at the age of 89.

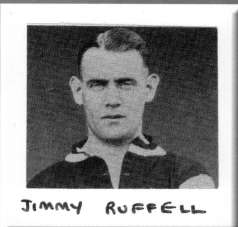

JIMMY RUFFELL

PAOLO DI CANIO (1999-2003)
Appearances: 141
Goals: 51

A passionate Italian forward who played with his heart on his sleeve, Paolo Di Canio became a hugely popular figure during his four-and-a-half year stay with West Ham United. Signed from Sheffield Wednesday in January 1999, Rome-born Di Canio made his Hammers debut in a goalless Premier League draw at Wimbledon that month.

West Ham would finish the 1998/99 season in fifth place, with Di Canio scoring four goals to help the club qualify for the UEFA Intertoto Cup. The following season, Di Canio scored the Goal of the Season with a spectacular volley in the 2-1 victory over Wimbledon at the Boleyn Ground.

The Italian was voted Hammer of the Year in 2000. Never far from the limelight, Di Canio also hit the headlines when he scored a dramatic winner at Old Trafford in the 1-0 FA Cup fourth-round win over Manchester United in January 2001.

ANSWERS

HAMMERS QUIZ ANSWERS (pg31)

1. Thames Ironworks FC
2. Syd King
3. 1919
4. Billie
5. Vic Watson
6. Bobby Moore OBE
7. John Sissons, Sir Geoff Hurst MBE, Ron Boyce
8. TSV 1860 Munich
9. Bobby Moore OBE, Sir Geoff Hurst MBE, Martin Peters MBE
10. Alan Taylor

WORDSEARCH ANSWERS (pg14)

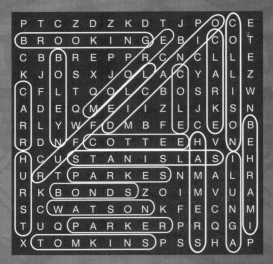

SPOT THE DIFFERENCE (pg48)

LUIS JIMENEZ